BASEBALL LEGENDS

Hank Aaron
Grover Cleveland Alexander
Ernie Banks
Albert Belle
Johnny Bench
Yogi Berra
Barry Bonds
Roy Campanella
Roberto Clemente
Ty Cobb
Dizzy Dean
Joe DiMaggio
Bob Feller
Jimmie Foxx
Lou Gehrig
Bob Gibson
Ken Griffey, Jr.
Rogers Hornsby
Walter Johnson
Sandy Koufax
Greg Maddux
Mickey Mantle
Christy Mathewson
Willie Mays
Stan Musial
Satchel Paige
Mike Piazza
Cal Ripken, Jr.
Brooks Robinson
Frank Robinson
Jackie Robinson
Babe Ruth
Tom Seaver
Duke Snider
Warren Spahn
Willie Stargell
Frank Thomas
Honus Wagner
Ted Williams
Carl Yastrzemski
Cy Young

CHELSEA HOUSE PUBLISHERS

BASEBALL LEGENDS

KEN GRIFFEY, JR.

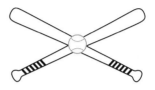

Lois P. Nicholson

Introduction by
Jim Murray

Senior Consultant
Earl Weaver

CHELSEA HOUSE PUBLISHERS
Philadelphia

EL DORADO COUNTY LIBRARY
345 FAIR LANE
PLACERVILLE, CA 95667

Cover photo credit: AP/Wide World Photo

Produced by Choptank Syndicate, Inc.

Editor and Picture Researcher: Norman L. Macht
Production Coordinator and Editorial Assistant: Mary E. Hull
Designer: Lisa Hochstein
Cover Designer: Alison Burnside

Copyright © 1997 by Chelsea House Publishers,
a division of Main Line Book Co. Printed and
bound in the United States of America.

1 3 5 7 9 8 6 4 2

Library of Congress Cataloging-in-Publication Data

Nicholson, Lois, 1949-
      ·Ken Griffey, Jr. / Lois P. Nicholson; introduction by Jim
Murray; senior consultant, Earl Weaver.
        p. cm. — (Baseball legends)
      Includes bibliographical references and index.
      Summary: A biography of the centerfielder who joined the
Seattle Mariners as the youngest player in the American League
in 1989, with the difficult task of living up to the
reputation of his famous father.
      ISBN 0-7910-4377-0 (hc)
      1. Griffey, Ken, Jr.—Juvenile literature. 2. Baseball
players—United States—Biography—Juvenile literature.
3. Seattle Mariners (Baseball team)—Juvenile literature.
[Griffey, Ken, Jr. 2. Baseball players. 3. Afro-Americans-   -Biography.] I. Weaver,
Earl, 1930- . II. Title.
III. Series.
GV865.G69N53 1997
796.357'092—dc21
[B]   97-8916
                                          CIP
                                         ·AC

CONTENTS

WHAT MAKES A STAR

Jim Murray

No one has ever been able to explain to me the mysterious alchemy that makes one man a .350 hitter and another player, more or less identical in physical makeup, hard put to hit .200. You look at an Al Kaline, who played with the Detroit Tigers from 1953 to 1974. He was pale, stringy, almost poetic-looking. He always seemed to be struggling against a bad case of mononucleosis. But with a bat in his hands, he was King Kong. During his career, he hit 399 home runs, rapped out 3,007 hits, and compiled a .297 batting average.

Form isn't the reason. The first time anybody saw Roberto Clemente step into the batter's box for the Pittsburgh Pirates, the best guess was that Clemente would be back in Double A ball in a week. He had one foot in the bucket and held his bat at an awkward angle—he looked as though he couldn't hit an outside pitch. A lot of other ballplayers may have had a better-looking stance. Yet they never led the National League in hitting in four different years, the way Clemente did.

Not every ballplayer is born with the ability to hit a curveball. Nor is exceptional hand-eye coordination the key to heavy hitting. Big league locker rooms are filled with players who have all the attributes, save one: discipline. Every baseball man can tell you a story about a pitcher who throws a ball faster than anyone has ever seen but who has no control on or *off* the field.

The Hall of Fame is full of people who transformed themselves into great ballplayers by working at the sport, by studying the game, and making sacrifices. They're overachievers—and winners. If you want to find them, just watch the World Series. Or simply read about New York Yankee great Lou Gehrig; Ted Williams, "the Splendid Splinter" of the Boston Red Sox; or the Dodgers' strikeout king Sandy Koufax.

A pitcher *should* be able to win a lot of ballgames with a 98-miles-per-hour fastball. But what about the pitcher who wins 20 games a year with a fastball so slow that you can catch it with your teeth? Bob Feller of the Cleveland Indians got into the Hall of Fame with a blazing fastball that glowed in the dark. National League star Grover Cleveland Alexander got there with a pitch that took considerably longer to reach the plate; but when it did arrive, the pitch was exactly where Alexander wanted it to be—and the last place the batter expected it to be.

There are probably more players with exceptional ability who didn't make it to the major leagues than there are who did. A number of great hitters, bored with fielding practice, had to be dropped from their team because their home-run production didn't make up for their lapses in the field. And then there are players like Brooks Robinson of the Baltimore Orioles, who made himself into a human vacuum cleaner at third base because he knew that working hard to become an expert fielder would win him a job in the big leagues.

A star is not something that flashes through the sky. That's a comet. Or a meteor. A star is something you can steer ships by. It stays in place and gives off a steady glow; it is fixed, permanent. A star works at being a star.

And that's how you tell a star in baseball. He shows up night after night and takes pride in how brightly he shines. He's Willie Mays running so hard his hat keeps falling off; Ty Cobb sliding to stretch a single into a double; Lou Gehrig, after being fooled in his first two at-bats, belting the next pitch off the light tower because he's taken the time to study the pitcher. Stars never take themselves for granted. That's why they're stars.

1

REFUSE TO LOSE

"It felt like a war out there."
— Don Mattingly

Ken Griffey, Jr. stood on first base, hands on hips, gazing over at Joey Cora on third. He had just smoked a single to center field in the bottom of the 11th inning to bring the Seattle Mariners within one run of tying the Yankees in the final game of the 1995 AL division playoffs. An entire season had come down to this one game on Sunday, October 8. The winners would go on to face the Cleveland Indians for the American League pennant and a trip to the World Series. The losers would go home.

The game, like the entire series, had been an epic dogfight with both teams exchanging the lead repeatedly throughout each contest. Griffey's eighth-inning home run off New York's ace hurler David Cone had put Seattle ahead 4–3. It was his fifth round-tripper of the series, tying the post-season record.

Despite Griffey's go-ahead blast in the eighth, the Yankees battled back once more to overtake the Mariners for the third time that night in the top of the 11th.

Now Cora, standing on third, represented the Mariners' tying run; Griffey, on first, the winning

Ken Griffey, Jr. smiles from beneath a pile of his team-mates who mobbed him after he scored the winning run in the bottom of the 11th inning against the New York Yan-kees October 8, 1995 in Seattle. The Mariners advanced to the ALCS for the first time in their history. Coach Sam Perlozzo said Grif-fey's grin was "the biggest smile I ever saw on a man's face."

run with no outs. Edgar Martinez stepped into the batter's box to face "Black Jack" McDowell on the mound. Neither McDowell nor Seattle's Randy Johnson had pitched from the bullpen during the entire season, but both ace starters were now in this do-or-die struggle.

An entire nation sat riveted in front of their televisions watching with the 57,411 fans in the Kingdome, many wearing T-shirts bearing the Mariners battle cry, "Refuse to Lose." Seattle fans had waited 19 years for this moment. Not only had the Mariners never made it to postseason play, their club had enjoyed only two winning seasons since they joined the league in 1976.

Griffey, 25, the son of former major leaguer Ken Griffey, Sr., had joined the Mariners as a highly-touted 19-year-old rookie in 1989. The kid had not disappointed. He had quickly become one of the best in the game. Each year his home run count had grown along with his popularity. His name had been linked with the game's immortals like Ruth, Mantle and Mays. Yet one key factor separated him from this elite group: until now he had played for losing teams.

Just a year earlier, Griffey had considered leaving the Mariners. He had questioned his teammates' desire to be champions, openly wondering if they had the "heart " to win. Now they had answered him. And they had done it largely without him.

On May 26 Griffey had broken his left wrist when he crashed into the wall while making a spectacular catch at the Kingdome. Doctors said his wrist " just exploded" when he hit the fence. It took surgeons three hours to repair the damage using a metal plate and seven screws to hold the shattered wrist together. Seattle's big gun missed 73 games.

"His getting hurt really helped the team," coach Sam Perlozzo said later, "and it took pressure off him. The other players realized that they were part of the team and it wasn't just the Griffey Mariners."

Still, when Griffey returned to action on August 24, the Mariners trailed the red-hot California Angels by 11 1/2 games. That night Griffey announced his return by hitting a game-winning ninth-inning home run to beat the Yankees. Then the Mariners got hot while the Angels cooled. In the midst of a 16 and 3 stretch, they caught the Angels and took over first place. But the teams finished in a tie for first in the AL West, forcing a one-game playoff at the Kingdome. Seattle won it, 9–1, to earn a shot at the Yankees, winners of the East Division title.

Sam Perlozzo recalled, "About a week before the season ended, and the fight for the playoff spot was still on, and Junior's wrist was still not

Seattle DH Edgar Martinez drives in the winning run in the the playoffs against the Yankees. In 1995 Martinez won his second AL batting title with a .358 average, the highest by a right-hand hitter in the league in 56 years.

one hundred percent, he was standing back of the batting cage and he said to some of the other Mariners, 'You guys play well and get us there, and then you can all jump on my shoulders.'

"That was a bold statement for a youngster to make. A lot of stars never get to postseason play and you wonder how they would do under that pressure. He showed what he could do."

The favored Yankees won the first two games in New York, despite three home runs by Griffey. But the tide turned when the series resumed in Seattle, the Mariners winning the next two. Each game had been a battle, a wild roller coaster ride with momentum swinging back and forth between the clubs from inning to inning.

Seattle's rookie shortstop Alex Rodriguez leaps into Ken Griffey's arms after the Mariners' upset win over the Yankees. The next year Rodriguez, 20, would blossom into a superstar.

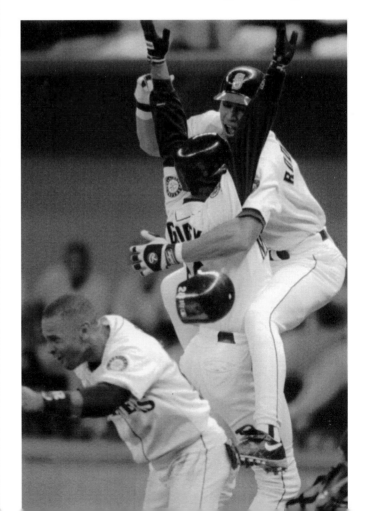

In the showdown, the Mariners trailed 3–2 in the ninth, but filled the bases on two walks and a single. With the count 3–2 on Doug Strange, New York's ace David Cone missed with a forkball to force home the tying run. As Cone doubled over, hanging his head in frustration, Yankees manager Buck Showalter summoned his final weapon from the bullpen, McDowell. The game went into extra innings.

After New York took the lead off Randy Johnson in the top of the 11th, Joey Cora opened the bottom of the inning with a bunt single. Griffey singled him to third. Edgar Martinez lined a shot down the left field line, scoring Cora. Perlozzo, coaching at third, started to hold Griffey up. But here came Griffey running faster than the coach had ever seen him run, so Perlozzo waved him on.

Griffey slid home with the winning run, and was buried under a joyous mound of hugging Mariners as fireworks erupted and 57,000 fans screamed and cheered. The Yankees sat in stunned silence before slowly filing into the clubhouse where their captain, Don Mattingly, told reporters, "It felt like a war out there."

Ken Griffey, Jr. had not only realized his dream of playing on a winning team, he had also saved the Mariners for Seattle. Following almost two decades of losers, the owners had planned to move the financially troubled franchise. But the winning season had changed their minds and made a new stadium feasible. Seattle fans would keep the Mariners, thanks to the team that refused to lose.

2

GROWING UP IN BASEBALL

"How positive are you about yourself?"
— Ken Griffey, Sr.

George Kenneth Griffey, Jr. was born on November 21, 1969 in Donora, a town of 7,500 in western Pennsylvania, and the birthplace of Hall of Famer Stan Musial. Junior's grandfather, Buddy Griffey, had been Musial's teammate at Donora High long before the future slugger would star with the St. Louis Cardinals. Musial remembered Buddy Griffey as a left-handed third baseman and the school's football star.

Buddy Griffey had abandoned his wife, Ruth, and six children when the children were young. Ruth worked odd jobs to provide for the family, but occasionally they had to rely on welfare to make ends meet.

Ken Senior's childhood memories included stuffing the soles of his worn out shoes with cardboard before walking five miles to play baseball with friends. When he was old enough, he worked in a grocery store and then in a steel factory making bombs for the Vietnam war. His least favorite job was reading meters for the local electric company. Dogs chased him; he carried six cans of Mace spray to protect himself. It was not

They called Pete Rose "Charlie Hustle" because he went all-out on every play. Here he tangles with Bud Harrelson of the Mets after they collided on a play at second base. Rose played with Ken Griffey, Sr., on the 1975 and 1976 World Champion Cincinnati Reds. Ken, Jr. played with Rose's son in the Reds' clubhouse.

fun, but it may have helped his future base-running skills.

Ken married Alberta "Birdie" Littleton after they graduated from high school, where he had been an All-State end on the football team, and she had excelled at basketball and volleyball.

Following Junior's birth, the family moved to Cincinnati, Ohio. Senior had just been drafted by the Reds. Although his minor league salary was only $500 a month, the family went with him wherever he played. This was important to him. Ken, Sr. vowed that he would be a good parent and spend time with his family, which grew to include Craig in 1970 and Lathesia in 1972.

Senior worked his way up through the Reds organization and reached the big leagues in 1973. In 1975 he became the regular right fielder. He was a consistent .300 hitter and the fastest runner in the league. His enthusiasm for the game and enjoyment of playing ball showed on and off the field. Led by manager Sparky Anderson, the Big Red Machine won the World Series in 1975 and 1976.

Like his father, Junior loved the game and showed early promise as an athlete. While most babies take their first steps at about the age of 1, Junior walked when he was only 7 months old. He was playing baseball when he was 4, but his father let him develop slowly. "I don't believe in pressuring kids," he said. "I told the boys, 'If you want to play, and you need some help, please let me know.' With Junior, you could see it was what he wanted and how much fun he was having playing it."

Junior hung out at Riverfront Stadium with the Reds players and the sons of Cincinnati stars Pete Rose, Hal McRae, Tony Perez and Lee May. Reds equipment manager Bernie Stowe sometimes wondered if he was running a clubhouse or a childcare facility. Like all kids, they got into mischief, swiping candy from the team's stock. "Eduardo Perez was the only kid who could reach the shelf," Stowe recalled. "He and the Juniors [Pete Rose, Jr. and Ken Griffey, Jr.] were all six or seven years old and did not know better, but they thought they were sly. While the two Juniors staked out the door to the laundry room, Eduardo raided the candy. They'd fill their pockets and take off."

When Ken Griffey, Sr. was traded to the New York Yankees in 1981, the move took him away from home for the first time. Junior's mother, Birdie, became the chief coach and cheerleader for her sons at their Little League and high school games.

Ken, Jr. sat on Sparky Anderson's lap during interviews, and helped himself to the sodas in the manager's refrigerator. But the future Hall of Famers like Rose, Johnny Bench and Joe Morgan did not awe him. "They were just people my dad worked with," he recalled. "I didn't walk around thinking, 'Wow, these are the Cincinnati Reds.' My dad told me, 'Don't copy them. Just be yourself.'"

Nor did Junior see his father as a big star. "When he came home, he was just like any other father coming home. I was like any kid. I wanted to play catch with him. He'd play catch with me and with all the other kids in the neighborhood."

Occasionally Birdie would join them in the backyard. "She used to play catch with me," Junior recalled. "But one day I threw hard and smoked her hand. She threw down the glove, and that was the last time she caught for me."

When he was 8, Junior pitched and played outfield for Mt. Airy in the Class D Knothole League. His brother, Craig, was also on the team. At first his father stressed the mental part of the game. He asked questions like, "How positive are you about yourself . . . How much confidence do you have in yourself and what you want to do?" He told Junior that no one was ever going to hit, run or throw for him; he had to do it for himself.

Junior seemed to be blessed with a smooth, natural swing. But he worked for hours on his defense by throwing a ball high in the air and running under it to catch it with both hands. "That's how I learned to go back after a fly ball," he later explained. "I go back a lot better than I come in. I've always felt more comfortable going back."

By the time Junior was 11, his father could no longer strike him out. But for all his confidence, Junior had difficulty controlling his emotions. Once he smacked a hard shot that was snared by the first baseman. He cried so hard they had to take him out of the game. His mother tried to comfort him, reminding him that his father also made outs. "One out is not going to make any difference," she said.

Still sobbing, he replied, "But that's him, that's not me."

Later, Junior remembered his father's advice about not taking the game too seriously. "Dad always used to tell me to go out and have fun, no matter what. I never saw him upset when he was in the outfield."

In the fall of 1981, less than three weeks before Junior's twelfth birthday, the Reds traded Senior to the New York Yankees. Cincinnati was home; New York was a foreign land. Life would change drastically for the entire Griffey family.

For Junior and Craig, Riverfront Stadium was no longer their second home. Once spring training began, they would not see their father until school was out. Suddenly, their close relationship with him depended on telephones and airplanes.

3

BECOMING AN ATHLETE

"My parents told me from the beginning,
I could be a ballplayer or I could be
a what-if."

— Ken Griffey, Jr.

Young Ken Griffey dominated Cincinnati Little League, getting a hit almost every time he batted. He was so good the other coaches refused to believe he was only 11 years old and demanded to see his birth certificate. He made his own coach so angry by ignoring all advice, the coach threw him off the team.

"I had a father in the big leagues and this Little League coach was telling me how to hit," Junior recalled. "After the team lost a couple of games, they asked me back. The coach knew he was wrong."

In Senior's absence, Birdie took over. She drove her sons to the games in the family Rolls Royce and became the chief cheerleader and coach. She sent her husband detailed accounts of each game. Occasionally, Senior requested a face-to-face session with Junior.

"If I did something wrong on the field, he would fly me to New York," Junior said. "He'd tell me what I should have done. Then he would send me home the next day, and I'd play baseball."

Ken Griffey, Sr. is caught in a "pickle" or rundown in a 1985 game. An All-Star outfielder with exceptional speed, he and Junior became the first father and son team to play in the big leagues at the same time.

Once when he was 14 Junior did a little hot dogging, and he heard about it from his father. He hit a home run and waved his arms in the air as he rounded the bases. After a stern lecture, he didn't do that anymore.

Misbehaving at home would often lead to a plane ride to New York. But Junior soon learned that this could be more of a reward than a punishment. Senior remembered that "the first time he thought he was going to get a whuppin' I told him, 'You ready to go?'

"'Where are we gonna go?' Junior asked.

"I said, 'We're going to the stadium. If you want to go hit, you can hit.'

"After that he did a couple bad things because he knew they'd send him to me, and he was going to the stadium to hit."

During summer trips to New York the Griffey brothers played with the kids of their father's teammates at the stadium. Yankee Hall of Famer Phil Rizzuto remembered them playing pickle (rundowns between the bases) in the hallway outside the clubhouse. At times they created such a commotion they were ejected. The Yankees' Willie Randolph said, "He was always running around, zipping here and there, never still. Players would tell him, 'Slow down. You're making me dizzy!' And he always had a big smile on his face, having fun."

By the 1985 season Junior's swaggering presence on the field made an impression on the big leaguers. "He knew how good he was," said one. Hall of Famer Yogi Berra, then a New York coach, watched him launch rockets into the bleachers during batting practice and extolled him to visitors.

Outfielder Rickey Henderson joined the Yankees that season and quickly became Junior's favorite player. Known for his speed on the bases, Henderson sported number 24 on his pinstripes, the same number that Junior later chose when he entered the major leagues. Henderson took an interest in Junior, often playing one-on-one basketball with him. He also gave him advice that Junior never forgot.

"He told me, 'You're going to be here in the majors someday,'" Ken remembered. "Stay away from the wrong crowds. If somebody does drugs, his name may not be mentioned, but yours will."

Junior heeded Henderson's advice. "I've always been able to stay away from that stuff," he said. "My parents told me from the beginning, I could be a ballplayer or I could be a what-if. I have pride in myself, pride in my family, and pride in my teammates. I wouldn't want to do anything to jeopardize any of those three."

The hot-tempered Billy Martin returned as the Yankees manager that season. One day the team was taking a pounding, and some of the players' kids opted for a game of dodge ball in the clubhouse during the game.

Martin was particularly upset with Senior's poor performance that day. When he saw the kids playing in the clubhouse, he ordered just the Griffey kids to leave. When Senior learned what had happened he was livid, but he later urged them to forget it. From that day, Junior refused to go back to Yankee Stadium until he returned as a professional.

Despite his athletic skills, Junior did not play sports during his first two years at Archbishop Moeller High in Cincinnati. His mother called him a "lazy student"; his poor grades prevented him from playing as a freshman. The following year he chose to accompany his father to Florida for spring training instead of playing high school

Rickey Henderson took a special interest in the teen-age Junior in 1985, advising him to stay away from drugs and the wrong crowds. The game's premier leadoff man, Henderson holds the record of 130 stolen bases in a season.

baseball. His father warned him, "Do you want to make something of yourself, or do you want to end up like so many of your friends in high school, the ones who don't have a job and are still living at home."

For his sixtienth birthday, Junior's parents gave him a $30,000 BMW. Junior later admitted that he was spoiled. But when he got a ticket for speeding, his parents pulled in the reins on him.

Now 6-foot-2 and weighing 180 pounds, Junior played football that fall as a wide receiver for Moeller's state champions. But he did not like being tackled and risking an injury that might hurt his baseball career, so he never played football again.

In the spring of 1986 he made the varsity baseball team for the first time. The coach, Mike Cameron, had heard all the rumors about what a great player Kenny was, so he was surprised when the great Griffey swung at the first 10 pitches he saw and missed every one. "That's terrible," Cameron said to the young slugger. "You missed every pitch. That swing will have to go."

"Nah," replied the confident Kenny. "That's the Griffey swing."

During his 20 years as a coach at Moeller, Cameron had tutored several future big league stars, including Cincinnati shortstop Barry Larkin. But he had never seen anyone like young Griffey. Junior's hitting skills improved so dramatically that soon Coach Cameron declined to pitch to him during batting practice. The kid hit the ball so hard that "even with a screen up in front of the mound, his bat speed was so great that he was intimidating," said Cameron.

"With all kids, I really believe that, until they fail, they'll never listen to you," he said. "And Kenny had never met failure. When kids start failing they come up to you and say, 'Coach, what am I doing wrong?' Then you know they're ready to listen. I knew I would never see the time when Kenny would ask me that."

Agreeing with Cameron's assessment, Junior said, "No, I didn't ask him for help. Anything he said I had heard from my father since I was 9 years old."

But whenever his father got to see him play, it had a negative effect on him. "Only when his father was there would Kenny pressure himself," Cameron said. "A hundred scouts could be in the stands, and it wouldn't make a difference. But not his father."

Junior admitted, "When he was there, it was the only time I thought I had to impress somebody. He'd say he was the one guy I didn't have to impress."

When he was 16 Junior played in a Connie Mack league with 18-year-olds and led his team to the World Series, where he hit three home runs. The next year he repeated as Moeller's Player of the Year, batting .478.

On June 2, 1987, the Seattle Mariners made him their first selection in the amateur draft. "He has speed, power and a good arm," they said, rating him as the player with the best overall potential in the draft. With his father acting as his agent, the 17-year-old received a $160,000 bonus. Seattle assigned him to Bellingham in the Class A Northwest League and told him, "We want you in the majors in three years."

4

"IT'S GRIFFEY TIME"

"I wasn't prepared for it."
— Ken Griffey, Jr.

The bush leagues were a wake-up call for the kid from Cincinnati who later admitted, "I wasn't prepared for it." Until then, he had led the good life, outplaying all his peers on the field, driving his own BMW, and flying around the country to visit his father.

Now Griffey found himself in Bellingham, Washington, a town of 46,380 people about 90 miles north of Seattle. Conditions in the minor leagues surprised him. His team often played games in the neighboring states of Oregon and Idaho, requiring 10-hour bus rides in a 30-year-old bus with no bathroom. During these grueling bus trips Griffey usually climbed into the luggage rack and tried to sleep as the ramshackle vehicle made its long, rough journeys over the mountains. He also had several run-ins with the sons of the team's bus driver when they called him "nigger."

In his first at-bat Griffey was fooled and took a called third strike. The pitcher had thrown a forkball, a pitch that sinks sharply. Despite all the years spent with his father in the majors, he later explained, "I had never seen one before."

The same young man who had walked with a swagger around big league ballparks rubbing

Blessed with a natural effortless batting stroke, Ken Griffey needed no coaching in hitting. His talent made him a little lazy, and an attack of homesickness made his first year in the minor leagues an unhappy one.

elbows with the game's stars contracted a common malady of minor leaguers. He was homesick. "To be honest with you, it was a whole lot worse than I ever imagined," Griffey later said. "I kept thinking about things I'd be doing back at home. You know, running around the house with my brother, being at the pool, just things like that. I didn't know what to do. All I knew was I wanted to go home."

Griffey was not hustling and he lazily snagged fly balls with one hand. He made mental errors. His manager, Rick Sweet, told a reporter, "He's been picked off base twice already because he's been spectating [watching the game from a spectator's perspective while playing]. He's got to stay ahead mentally. You can't spectate in this game."

Long distance phone calls to his parents increased; soon the Griffeys' monthly phone bills

Rick Sweet was Griffey's first professional manager. A former catcher, Sweet played hard. He did not appreciate Griffey's nonchalant attitude and mental errors on the field. "You can't spectate in this game," he told Griffey.

reached $600. But things only worsened as Griffey fell into a slump, batting .230. Alberta flew to Bellingham to visit her homesick son. When she arrived she was surprised to learn that Griffey had been benched for breaking a team curfew.

Alberta Griffey's patience had worn as thin as the hide on a baseball. "I knew he needed some sympathy, but I got mad and told him to concentrate on his career," she remembered. "The night before I left, I gave it to him up one side and down the other. He didn't call me for four days."

Whatever Alberta said, her words hit the mark. Soon Griffey came out of his nose dive, batting .450. When the season ended, he was sent to the Instructional League in Arizona, where each major league team sent its six best minor league players.

Griffey returned to Cincinnati in December when the Instructional League's season concluded. Senior talked with his son about being self-reliant, suggesting that he pay his parents rent or think about moving out and getting his own place.

Following six months of criticism in the minors, Griffey considered his father's advice as more negative judgment. "It seemed like everyone was yelling at me in baseball, then I came home and everyone was yelling at me there," he remembered. "I got depressed. I got angry. I didn't want to live."

The following month, Griffey tried to end his life by swallowing 277 aspirin tablets. His girl-friend's mother drove him to nearby Providence Hospital in Mt. Airy where he was placed in intensive care. When his father heard the news he rushed to his son's bedside. The two began arguing. "I ripped the intravenous tubes out of my arm," Junior said. "That stopped his yelling."

The incident became public in 1992 when Griffey revealed the story to a Seattle newspaper. He hoped that disclosing the event would discourage others from attempting such an act. "Don't ever try to commit suicide," he said. "I am living proof of how stupid it is."

The 18-year-old began the 1988 season with the San Bernardino Spirit of the Class A California League. Most of his teammates were 21. Griffey struggled at first, going hitless in 17 consecutive at-bats. When he had an off day, he flew home to visit his mother, whose words again worked magic. He returned to San Bernardino and got 20 hits in his next 30 at-bats.

He was such a popular player that the team held a Ken Griffey, Jr. Poster Night promotion and packed Fiscalini Field. The public address announcer began introducing the hot young slugger, "Yes indeedy, boys and girls, what time is it?"

"It's Griffey time!" the fans screamed in unison.

On June 9 Junior strained his back stretching to make a diving catch and made the first of many journeys to the disabled list. When he returned on August 15, the Mariners promoted him to their AA team in Vermont. Despite his ailing back he batted .444 and led the team with 7 RBI in the Eastern League playoffs.

Griffey went to spring training with the Mariners in 1989 determined to make the team. He impressed manager Jim Lefebvre when, after fanning on three straight forkballs in a practice game, he lined the next forkball he saw down the third base line.

The Mariners realized his potential stardom, but they were cautious about rushing him. Other talented players had been set back a few years by bringing them up too fast.

Some coaches were concerned that Griffey would be pressured to live up to his father's reputation. "It's tough for a young kid to live up to or top those expectations," explained Mike Hegan, son of major league catcher Jim Hegan. "You put pressure on yourself to succeed and hope that you're not there because of your last name."

Griffey tried to be cool about it. "I'll be upset if I don't make it, but it's up to them and I won't cause problems," he told a writer. "I feel I can play every day right now even though I know I still have lots to learn. I am a little amazed I've come this far this fast."

On March 29, Lefebvre called the young rookie to his office. "This is the most difficult decision a manager has to make," he said. "I've talked to the coaches and we've considered a lot of things. You've made the team. Congratulations! You're my starting center fielder."

Later Griffey described how he felt when he heard those words. "My heart started ticking again. Those are probably the best words I've ever heard. At least in the top three."

He was 19 and he had already made it to The Show. Now he had to prove that he belonged there.

5

"WONDER BOY"

"Hitting is as simple as you want to make it."
— Ken Griffey, Jr.

When Ken Griffey, Jr. opened the season with Seattle in April 1989, it was the first time in the major leagues that a father and son had ever played at the same time. Senior had rejoined the Reds following the 1987 season. At 19, Griffey was also the youngest player in the majors.

Like most teens he dressed very casually, but the Mariners had a team rule prohibiting players from wearing jeans and sneakers on road trips. Birdie shopped for his travel wardrobe: a suit, three pairs of dress pants, sweaters, and two pairs of shoes. She drove his car to Seattle and got him an apartment. Realizing that her son would be paid twice a month, she hired an accountant to monitor his money and send one check home each month to put in his savings.

On April 3, Griffey played in his first major league game against the A's in Oakland, California. Facing the veteran Dave Stewart in his first at-bat, the rookie took the first pitch before stroking a fastball off the right field wall for a double. Senior had played earlier that day in Cincinnati and was able to watch his son's debut on television. First the TV showed Senior in his Reds uniform in 1975. Then it

Griffey never lets a wall stop him from robbing hitters of base hits and home runs. As a result, his aggressiveness has cost him playing time from broken bones.

showed Junior wearing the Mariners' blue and green. Senior later admitted that he cried watching it.

Junior did not get a hit in his next 18 at-bats, but he remained calm. "The only thing we don't know about him is how he will face that eight-to-nine game slump," said Mariners outfielder Jeffrey Leonard. "It's going to come, so we have to wait and see how he handles it."

"I just try not to worry about anything," Griffey said. "You know what they say, you shouldn't get too high or too low." And as he did in the minors, he spent as much as four hours a day talking to his parents, his brother Craig, and his girlfriend, Missy Parrett, in Cincinnati.

Junior hit his first big league home run on the first pitch he saw in the Kingdome on April 10, his father's birthday. Ten days later, Senior had a day off, and he and Birdie traveled to Chicago to see Junior at Comiskey Park. Birdie told reporters, "I'm treating this like a Little League game. That way, I'm not as nervous as I should be."

But Senior was not so calm. "I'm nervous. My palms are sweaty. I never dreamed about this happening, " he told the press. "I figured that when he signed with the Mariners, it would take at least four years for him to reach the majors."

Griffey made his parents' trip worthwhile by getting a tie-breaking single in the seventh inning, sparking a 5-2 Mariners victory.

In one stretch in April he made eight straight hits, convincing other players that he was no fluke. He did not care who was pitching, even when left-handers gave him problems. "How am I supposed to know who's pitching," he told a reporter. "I couldn't care less. He's still forced to throw me something I can hit. It just adds more pressure to know what a guy throws. You start looking for this or that and all of a sudden he's snuck a thirty-seven-mile-an-hour fastball by you."

"He's not a student of the game," his father explained. "He plays on instinct and ability and sometimes very little else."

But in many ways his entire childhood had been spent as a student of the game, absorbing it from big leaguers around him. He had developed a balanced batting stance, his feet slightly wider than his shoulders, weight evenly distributed, "like you're stepping on eggs," he put it. He kept his head still, eye on the ball, and swung in an arc that curved down, then up.

"Hitting is as simple as you make it," he said. "I don't think about hands, feet, alignment . . . Your hands will automatically take you where the ball is going. You can hold the bat any way you want. Just be comfortable . . . I just try to see it and hit it."

His outfield play also made the highlight films, the result of years of drills to sharpen his reaction time. Coaches would hit fungos while yelling, "Okay, left" or "Okay, right" and he would break in that direction while positioning himself to make the play. Veteran outfielder Willie Stargell had taught him to place the foot on the glove side of his body in front when fielding a ball. "When you come up with the ball, you'll be in a position to step and throw," Griffey explained. He made leaping catches before crashing into walls and diving grabs off the grass.

"A lot of times I think he's going to come back down to reality," said right fielder Jay Buhner.

Right fielder Jay Buhner is one of Griffey's closest friends and greatest admirers on the Mariners. Batting behind Griffey in the lineup, he often forces pitchers to pitch to Griffey rather than face the menacing Buhner.

"But then he'll climb the wall and make an incredible catch that nine out of 10 center fielders wouldn't have even tried for."

Once in the bottom of the ninth of a tie game at Fenway Park, Boston's Wade Boggs hit a ball to deep left center field. The drive seemed to have triple stamped all over it. Griffey dashed after it, leaped and caught the ball just before he crashed into the outfield wall. He fell to the grass and lay still for an instant before lifting his glove to show he had snared the seed. The Red Sox fans cheered in appreciation of the breathtaking play.

Another time his father was in the stands to see him play at Yankee Stadium. In the fourth inning New York hitter Jesse Barfield launched a long shot to left center. Sprinting like a gazelle, Griffey made his way back to the warning track, glanced at the wall, and leaped toward the sky. The Seattle pitchers in the bullpen behind the fence saw an arm extend three feet over the wall. They watched the ball hit the glove and the arm disappear, robbing Barfield of a home run.

Senior sat and stared in disbelief. "That had to be at least 400 feet away," he shouted.

A woman seated behind him leaned over and said, "Is that your son?"

Senior nodded.

"Jesse Barfield's my husband," she said.

Suddenly the spotlight on him was constant and blinding. He may have been ready to play in the big leagues, but he was not ready for all the media attention. During one press conference, he was rude to reporters. One writer described him as nothing more than a spoiled brat. The Mariners, upset with him, began to limit his interviews on the road. "It hasn't gotten out of hand," said Lefebvre, "but it's something that could. We want Junior to stay focused on baseball."

His popularity soared. A card company produced a candy bar featuring 12 photos of him; in one month sales earned him $30,000. Next came Ken Griffey, Jr. T-shirts and posters.

But the fun-loving 19-year-old crown prince also earned the respect of the older players in the Seattle clubhouse in the only way that counted—with his bat and glove. They treated him like a little brother, who loved rap music so much he had a 22-speaker stereo system installed in his car. "They make the car vibrate," he said. "I love it."

Junior's good time came to a sudden end on July 25. He fell in the shower, breaking the little finger on his left hand, and was out for a month. Eager to win Rookie of the Year honors when he returned to the lineup, he started swinging for the fences every time up, trying to hit the ball 700 feet, and batted just .181 the rest of the year. Still, he finished with a .264 average, 16 home runs and 61 RBI.

"There's no telling what kind of numbers Ken will put up when he gets serious about the game," said batting coach Gene Clines. "I mean, I can't imagine anybody being as good at his age. I call him 'Wonder Boy.' The scary part is what he'll be accomplishing when he's 25 years old."

6

FATHER AND SON REUNION

"We were having such a great time playing together, being teammates, playing baseball."
— Ken Griffey, Jr.

Fans enjoy watching Griffey because he always appears to be having fun, even when he is being criticized. Here he shows off a pacifier given to him by coach Gene Clines, who accused Griffey of whining too much in spring training in 1992.

The 20-year-old Ken Griffey, Jr. was so good—and made everything look so easy—other players who had to work hard for whatever they achieved turned green with envy. His happy-go-lucky attitude on the field irritated older heads. One day against Detroit, he did not run hard to first base on a ground ball. His father's old manager at Cincinnati, Sparky Anderson, now the Tigers skipper, scolded him: "You're lucky your dad didn't see you when you weren't hustling. People pay money to see you play."

Another manager, irked by Junior's nonchalance and his mental mistakes, his cockiness, and his clowning during batting practice, told a writer, "I hate him . . . Twenty years ago, if he did some of the things he does now, he would have been hit in the head [beaned by opposing pitchers] five times by now."

But the fans loved him, and they elected him to the All-Star team for the first time in 1990. Meanwhile, his father was struggling, playing part-time for the Reds. In August the 40-year-old Ken, Sr. decided to hang up his spikes and retire. The

Mariners, sensing the drawing power of having father and son together in their outfield, quickly picked him up. But it was more than a publicity stunt; Senior still had the ability and leadership qualities to contribute to the team.

On August 31 Senior batted second and Junior third in the Seattle lineup, marking the first time a father and son had played on the same team in the major leagues. As a surprise, Birdie arranged for a television station to beam a message from Craig to the Kingdome. Craig was a cornerback on the Ohio State football team. When the Griffeys saw his face on the scoreboard screen, they looked like contestants in a grinning contest.

Always competitive, father and son made a bet before the game. The first one to get a hit would be treated to dinner. Senior collected the first hit, and Junior picked up the check that night. After the Mariners' 5–2 victory, Junior said, "I didn't know what to think. I wanted to cry or something. I just stood there and looked at him in left field."

On September 14 in Anaheim, Senior blasted a home run. "That's the way you do it," he gloated as his son met him at home plate. Then Junior stepped up to the plate and launched his own round-tripper.

"That was the best month I've had in the majors," Junior said when the season ended. "We could have lost all our games the rest of the season and I wouldn't care. We were having such a great time playing together, being teammates, playing baseball."

Junior batted .300 with 22 home runs, and became the second youngest player to win a Gold Glove.

The 1991 season promised to be a year filled with magic for both Griffeys. But on March 2 Senior injured his neck in an automobile accident, sidelining him for much of the season. The Mariners—and Junior—got off to a slow start. By the All-Star break Griffey was batting just .280. Seattle was in sixth place. "I was down on myself more than I'd ever been in the first two years," he reflected. "I wanted to win so bad, and when we didn't, it was like, 'Oh, no, not again.'"

Second baseman Harold Reynolds watched his once-loose teammate become increasingly tense. "Why are you putting so much pressure on yourself?" he asked Griffey. "Just relax and have fun, and it'll happen."

Griffey was stung out of his doldrums by a column in the Seattle *Times* written by Steve Kelley, who compared him to another number 24, Willie Mays. Kelley wrote:

"We have had great expectations for you, but now we're beginning to wonder. We don't see

Griffey's Louisville Sluggers, made especially for him by Hillerich & Bradsby, are double-dipped to form a thick coat of hard lacquer. "My bats are hard as a rock," he said. "Stand around the batting cage and you'll hear a louder crack."

the work habits of Willie Mays. We don't see the hunger that drove Mays into the Hall of Fame.

"We wonder what a player would be like with your talent and your father's hunger. Ken Griffey, Sr. runs harder to first base than you do. Willie Mays was a marvelously talented athlete, but he also worked incredibly hard. He studied the game. It seems as if you are getting by with just your talent.

"Will you settle for being a multimillionaire instead of a Hall of Famer? Maybe now it's time to go to work. Time to be more than just a good player. Time to be great. But some of us wonder if you want it enough."

Kelley's harsh words stunned Griffey. He requested a meeting with the writer that was described as "tearful."

"The article made me think about what I was doing," he said. "It made me think, not about being great, but being the person I can be and what I want to accomplish in this game."

Griffey's two hits in the All-Star Game helped the American League defeat the Nationals. His performance skyrocketed for the remainder of the season. "Since that article was written, he's done a lot of great things," said manager Jim Lefebvre. "It set him on fire." He finished the season batting .327 with 22 homers and 100 RBIs, and won honors as the best offensive and defensive player.

The Mariners won 83 and lost 79 for their first winning season. Following surgery on his injured neck, Ken Griffey, Sr. retired and became the Seattle batting coach. The brief yet cherished time for father and son as teammates had ended. "I played baseball for nearly 20 years and playing with him was the number one memory of my career," Senior said. "The time I played with him was special; it was emotional for me. On the field I was his teammate, off the field I was his father, and on the bench I was his coach."

7

THE PAIN OF LOSING

"He can do things other guys can't do."
— Tino Martinez

Ken, Jr. and his brother Craig (right) were both drafted by the Mariners. Craig was a defensive back at Ohio State University before signing with Seattle in 1991. A speedy outfielder, he did not inherit the Griffey sweet swing.

Almost before the 1992 season got up a full head of steam, Ken Griffey, Jr. found himself on the disabled list again. On June 8 he dove for a fly ball in Texas and sprained his right wrist. He was out of action until June 25, when he signaled his return by homering on his first at-bat.

Now a perennial All-Star, he had three hits in the AL's 13–6 win and earned the game MVP Award, which his father had won in 1980.

Griffey put up his usual numbers for the year, but unfortunately so did the Mariners. They lost 98 games and finished seventh. When the season ended, Junior and Melissa Parrett were married.

Hoping to turn the team around, the Mariners hired Lou Piniella, who had played with Griffey Senior and had managed the Yankees and Reds, to lead the team. When asked how the new skipper and Junior would get along, Joe Morgan said, "Piniella is perfect for him. Lou knows what it takes to be a star and he's able to push him and keep him going. No matter who you are, every once in a while you need someone to put a burr under your saddle."

In 1993 Griffey's hitting exploded. On June 15 he became the sixth youngest player to reach 100 home runs. He was often walked intentionally and got angry when he was denied a chance to hit. His frustration built up until, one day against the Detroit Tigers, he got a decent pitch to hit and blasted it for a home run. Not satisfied, he made a rude gesture to manager Sparky Anderson in the Tigers dugout as he turned for home. Once again he had to apologize in public. "Everyone's done some things they regret," he said. "I've done my share too. The key is not to repeat your mistakes."

On July 20 Griffey started one of the hottest streaks in major league history, hitting a home run at Yankee Stadium. The next day he connected again. On July 25 he hit his sixth homer in as many games, and made it seven in a row with a grand slam at the Kingdome on July 27.

Every time he hit a homer, third base coach Sam Perlozzo would say, "You're the best, kid," as Griffey went by him.

Only two players had ever hit home runs in eight consecutive games: Dale Long of the Pittsburgh Pirates in 1956 and Yankee first baseman Don Mattingly in 1987. Mattingly had been Senior's teammate in New York. Now he watched

Ken Griffey, Jr. relaxes in the dugout with coaches Roman Mejias (left) and Sam Perlozzo (right) on Turn Back the Clock Night in 1994. Seattle's minor league team was called the Rainiers after nearby Mount Rainier before the city entered the American League in 1969.

Junior chase his record. "It's kind of funny," he said, "that this kid I watched shag fly balls and saw grow up has the chance to tie or possibly break the record."

Griffey tied the record with a Ruthian drive that hit the third tier of the Kingdome. Seattle fans gave him a three-minute standing ovation. First baseman Tino Martinez observed, "He can do things other guys can't do. He's playing way above everybody else in baseball right now." The next night Griffey had two hits but failed to reach the seats.

While some power hitters used bats weighing 33 to 35 ounces, Griffey preferred a 31-ounce piece of lumber. "A little bat, and bat control," he said. "I can pretty much stop my swing when I need to, unlike a 35-ounce bat where, once I let go, I've got no real control over it." Griffey's Louisville Sluggers, made especially for him by Hillerich & Bradsby, were double-dipped to coat them with a hard lacquer. "My bats are hard as a rock," he said. "Stand around the batting cage and you'll hear a louder crack."

Griffey's prowess with the bat proved that power hitters did not have to built like Frank Thomas, the White Sox' 6-foot-5, 257-pound first baseman, who was dubbed "The Big Hurt" and was Griffey's closest competitor for home run honors. "The other guys, all they have to do is use their big butts and big python arms to hit homers," Griffey said. "Me, I'm the little guy in the group. People always root for the little guy."

"The thing about Junior," Thomas said, "is he has that golden smile. He is like a kid on the sandlot. We're all competitors, we all play to win, but he always seems to be having more fun than the rest of us."

Seattle climbed to fourth in the standings on Griffey's 45 home runs and .309 batting average, and his Gold Glove play in the outfield.

The Griffeys' new year started in a big league way with the birth of their first child, Trey Kenneth, on January 19, 1994. Becoming a father

Griffey and his son, Trey, take part in a Mariners Family Day in 1995. With a longterm, multi-million dollar contract, Griffey owns a house in Seattle, a condominium in Cincinnati, 7 cars, 7 dogs, and a vast video game library. But, he says, playing baseball and his family make him happy, not the money.

was one of many changes Griffey faced as spring training approached. His father had left the Mariners, and the club was in a new division. Major league baseball had split each league into three divisions and expanded the playoffs to include one wild card team. Seattle was now in the AL West with California, Oakland and Texas.

Junior's brother, Craig, had been drafted by the Mariners in 1991. An outfielder, he struggled at bat and was still in the minor leagues five years later, batting .222. The two brothers played together once, in a split-squad practice game during spring training in 1994.

Talk of a players' strike cast a shadow over opening day, but it did not faze Griffey. By May 30 he had hit 22 home runs, a record for the first two months. But the team was playing poorly; in one stretch they lost 15 out of 20. Griffey grew increasingly frustrated and blasted his teammates publicly. "It takes heart to win and we don't have enough here to win the division. It's easier to roll over and quit. People say we've never won here and never will. For some players, it's easier to let it keep happening than to try to change it.

"I can't see staying. I hate to lose. I love Seattle and I love the people. But losing is killing me."

Griffey remained popular with fans of all ages, receiving a record 6 million All-Star votes. But baseball insiders continued to chafe at his light-hearted approach to the game. Just before the All-Star Game, Yankees manager Buck Showalter let loose a barrage of criticism. "I shouldn't say this publicly, but a guy like Ken Griffey, Jr., the game's boring to him. He comes on the field and his hat's on backward, his shirttail's hanging out. To me, that's a lack of respect for the game."

Using his bat to reply, Griffey won the home run contest. Then, wearing his hat backwards, he told reporters, "That's just me. I'm not going to change for anybody. Not serious about the game? I think my numbers have gone up each year."

The Mariners opened the second half of the season against the Yankees in Seattle. To show their support for Griffey, other Mariners wore their caps backwards during batting practice. The fans joined in, turning their caps around and booing the Yankee skipper.

Then the roof literally fell in. While the Yankees swept the series, some ceiling tiles fell from the Kingdome onto the seats and field. The club was forced to play their next 20 games on the road.

Griffey, wearing his cap backwards in his trademark style, talks hitting with White Sox first baseman Frank Thomas. Both sluggers had a chance to set home run records until a players' strike cut short the 1994 season.

On August 12 the entire roof caved in on baseball when the players went out on strike and the season ended with no playoffs and no World Series for the first time since 1905. For Griffey, going home early presented him with a more daunting task than hitting home runs. "You talk about the pressure of hitting home runs," he laughed. "I'd rather try to hit a home run than change my son's diaper any day. I get one leg down, the other one goes up. I get both legs down and all of a sudden, he's sitting up."

Griffey was leading the league with 40 home runs when the season was cut short with six weeks to go. White Sox slugger Frank Thomas had 39. Both had a chance to beat the record of 61 in a season, held by Roger Maris.

"We picked a bad year to have a good year," Griffey sighed.

8

THE YOUNG LEADER

"You never give up. Anything can happen."
— Ken Griffey, Jr.

Following their dramatic victory over the New York Yankees in the 1995 division series, the Mariners ran into the powerful Cleveland Indians and ran out of heroics. After winning two of the first three games in the ALCS, Seattle scored just two runs as the Indians took the last three games and the pennant.

On December 1 doctors removed the metal plate and seven screws from Griffey's injured wrist, but it would be another six months before it was completely healed.

The 1996 season was almost a duplicate of the year before, except for the ending. Griffey got off to a slow start—for him. By mid-May he had racked up 10 home runs, but he was batting around .250. Lingering effects of his wrist injury and a two-week bout of the flu and food poisoning hampered him. But his earlier injuries did not make him shy of the outfield fences. "When I play, I play hard," he said. "That's always been part of my game."

The Mariners' hopes were dealt a severe blow when the Big Unit, ace left-hander Randy Johnson, was lost for the year with back problems. And later in the year Griffey broke a bone in his left hand

Griffey enjoys visiting with youngsters more than dealing with adults. Although generous with his time and money, he faces more requests than he can possibly satisfy. "I sign as much as I can," he says, "but I can't sign for everybody."

that put him out for three weeks. Given up for lost, they fell 9 games back of the Texas Rangers with only 17 games to play. Then, like a champion racehorse sprinting from far back in the home stretch, they won 10 in a row while Texas slumped. The lead melted to 1 game. But they never got closer, falling back to finish 4 1/2 games out of the lead and 2 1/2 behind the wild card team, the Baltimore Orioles.

Griffey snared his seventh consecutive Gold Glove and wound up hitting .303 with career highs in home runs—49—and RBI—140.

Off the field it was a transition year for Griffey. Although he was only 26, he was no longer The Kid. He had been with the Mariners longer than all but two regulars, Jay Buhner and Edgar Martinez. During the season he proudly showed off photos of his eight-month-old daughter, Taryn, and boasted of the newest slugger in the family, two-year-old Trey.

In the clubhouse, where his locker was identified by one word—"Junior"—Griffey emerged as a leader, although his style was more fun-loving than firebrand. He did not get on other players, but spread enthusiasm instead. When the Mariners obtained Mark Whiten in a trade, Junior got him into a card game immediately to help him feel welcome. During the late-season 10-game winning streak, he was a cheerleader: "You never give up. Anything can happen."

His influence was especially felt by Seattle's 20-year-old shortstop sensation, Alex Rodriguez, who led the league with a .358 batting average. "I try to help him more off the field than on," Griffey said. "I told him just to make sure he has time for himself. I said, 'You're here to learn and have some fun. Don't worry about anything.'"

Griffey was happy to see the spotlight shift to the young Rodriguez. "There's no jealousy among us. I'm doing what I've always done, whatever I can to help the team win."

Griffey knew what the relentless demands of stardom were like. He could not visit a mall or go out to eat without being mobbed. On the road he played Nintendo in his room. He tried to complete his TV commercials before the season began. Before games, fans swarmed around the Seattle dugout wherever the team played, hoping to be one of the lucky few who would get a treasured Griffey autograph. "I sign as much as I can," he said, "but I can't sign for every-body." Like other stars, his haven was between the white lines. "From 5 p.m. until the game

At 26, Ken Griffey, Jr. became the Mariners' clubhouse leader. His influence was especially helpful to the club's 21-year-old shortstop sensation, Alex Rodriguez, who led the league with a .358 batting average in 1996.

Griffey's popularity and love for kids is similar to that of Babe Ruth, the game's most popular superstar of all time. Like Griffey, Ruth thrived on being surrounded by kids who idolized him. He never ducked a request to cheer up a sick child, usually without publicity.

ends, nobody bothers me. There are no phone calls. I just play and have fun."

Signed by the Mariners through 2000, Griffey seemed to be everywhere in the Northwest Empire. He had his own page on the World Wide Web, and answered readers' questions in a weekly newspaper column. His big smile glowed from TV commercials and posters. A Nike campaign promoted him as a candidate for president of the United States. He hosted an annual Christmas party for 350 inner-city youths, and used his $50,000 bonus for winning the Gold Glove to buy each one a gift. His $50,000 bonus for making the All-Star team went to take a group of children to Disneyland.

"He had as much fun as those kids," said Sam Perlozzo. "He was videotaping them and laughing and joking with them all day. Junior would rather deal with kids than adults any time. If you want him to meet some kids he'll be there in a second. But he'll shy away from meeting adults."

Through the lean years and the winning years Griffey's attitude on the field never changed. "Baseball is just a game," he said. "Play it, don't think about it."

Even the umpires noticed it. "His exuberance and having fun came across to the umpires," said veteran Jim Evans. "The success and the pressure that goes with it have not changed him. He enjoys what he is doing and it shows."

There seemed to be no limits to what Griffey could achieve. It depended on how long he chose to play. "As long as he enjoys it and he knows he can produce, I think he will play," Perlozzo said. "His pride will not let him continue if he cannot do the job any longer."

When his smile was no longer on his face as he swung the bat, that was when Ken Griffey, Jr. would be gone.

CHRONOLOGY

1969   Born George Kenneth Griffey, Jr. in Donora, Pennsylvania on November 21

1987   Bats .478 and is voted Player of the Year at Moeller High School and is drafted as first selection by the Seattle Mariners in the June amateur draft

1989   Hits a double in first major league at bat, April 3; hits first major league home run April 10

1990   Ken Griffey, Sr. signs with Mariners; he and Junior become first father and son to play on same major league team, on August 31
Becomes first Mariner elected to All-Star team
Wins first Gold Glove

1992   Named Most Valuable Player of All-Star Game
Marries Melissa Parrett

1993   Ties a major league record by hitting a home run in 8 straight games

1994   Son Trey Kenneth born on January 19

1995   Seattle Mariners reach playoffs for first time
Daughter Taryn Kennedy born October 21

1996   Wins seventh consecutive Gold Glove Award
Elected to All-Star team for seventh consecutive year

MAJOR LEAGUE STATISTICS

SEATTLE MARINERS

YEAR	TEAM	G	AB	R	H	2B	3B	HR	RBI	BA	SB
1989	SEA	127	455	61	120	23	0	16	61	.264	16
1990		155	597	91	179	23	0	16	61	.300	16
1991		154	548	76	179	42	1	22	100	.327	18
1992		142	565	83	174	39	4	27	103	.308	10
1993		156	582	113	180	38	3	45	109	.309	17
1994		111	433	94	140	24	4	40	90	.323	11
1995		72	260	52	67	7	0	17	42	.258	4
1996		140	545	125	165	26	2	49	140	.303	16
Totals		1057	3985	615	1204	227	21	238	725	.303	108

FURTHER READING

Ekin, Larry. *Baseball Fathers, Baseball Sons: From Orator Jim to Cal, Barry, and Ken. Every One A Player.* Cincinnati: Betterway Books, 1992.

Gowdey, David. *Baseball's Super Stars.* New York: Putnam, 1994.

Gutman, Bill, *Ken Griffey, Jr.* Brookfield, CT: Millbrook Press, 1993.

Kramer, Sydelle A. *Baseball's Greatest Hitters.* New York: Random Books for Young Readers, 1995.

Reiser, Howard. *The Kid.* Chicago: Children's Press, 1994.

Rolfe, John. *Ken Griffey, Jr. and Ken Griffey, Sr.* New York: Bantam, 1995.

INDEX

PICTURE CREDITS

National Baseball Library and Archives, Cooperstown, NY: pp. 2, 11, 23, 26, 28, 35, 55, 56; AP/World Wide Photos: pp. 8, 12, 17, 20, 32, 38, 44, 48, 50, 52, 58; Transcendental Graphics: p. 14; U. of Louisville: p. 41; Sam Perlozzo: p. 46

LOIS P. NICHOLSON is a native of Sudlersville, Maryland. She holds a bachelor's degree in education from Salisbury State University. She is a school library media specialist at Elkridge Elementary near Baltimore. In addition to Ken Griffey, Jr. she has written the following biographies for young readers: George Washington Carver: Botanist and Ecologist; Oprah Winfrey: Entertainer; Helen Keller; Michael Jackson; Casey Stengel; Nolan Ryan; Booker T. Washington (Chelsea House); Cal Ripken, Jr.: Quiet Hero (Tidewater); Georgia O'Keefe (Lucent); and Babe Ruth: Sultan of Swat (Goodwood Press). In addition to writing, Nicholson visits schools and speaks to students and faculties about writing nonfiction. She is the mother of two grown children and lives in Baltimore.

JIM MURRAY, veteran sports columnist of the *Los Angeles Times,* is one of America's most acclaimed writers. He has been named "America's Best Sportswriter" by the National Association of Sportscasters and Sportswriters 14 times, was awarded the Red Smith Award, and was twice winner of the National Headliner Award. In addition, he was awarded the J. G. Taylor Spink Award in 1987 for "meritorious contributions to baseball writing." With this award came his 1988 induction into the National Baseball Hall of Fame in Cooperstown, New York. In 1990, Jim Murray was awarded the Pulitzer Prize for Commentary.

EARL WEAVER is the winningest manager in the Baltimore Orioles' history by a wide margin. He compiled 1,480 victories in his 17 years at the helm. After managing eight different minor league teams, he was given the chance to lead the Orioles in 1968. Under his leadership the Orioles finished lower than second place in the American League East only four times in 17 years. One of only 12 managers in big league history to have managed in four or more World Series, Earl was named Manager of the Year in 1979. The popular Weaver had his number, 5, retired in 1982, joining Brooks Robinson, Frank Robinson, and Jim Palmer, whose numbers were retired previously. Earl Weaver continues his association with the professional baseball scene by writing, broadcasting, and coaching.